YOUR KNOWLEDGE HAS

Ninad Gondhalekar

Controlling the atmospheric turbulence, microPIC programming

GRIN Publishing

Bibliographic information published by the German National Library:

The German National Library lists this publication in the National Bibliography; detailed bibliographic data are available on the Internet at http://dnb.dnb.de .

Imprint:

Copyright © 2013 GRIN Verlag GmbH
Print and binding: Books on Demand GmbH, Norderstedt Germany
ISBN: 978-3-656-84504-1

This book at GRIN:

http://www.grin.com/en/e-book/284209/controlling-the-atmospheric-turbulence-micropic-programming

GRIN - Your knowledge has value

Since its foundation in 1998, GRIN has specialized in publishing academic texts by students, college teachers and other academics as e-book and printed book. The website www.grin.com is an ideal platform for presenting term papers, final papers, scientific essays, dissertations and specialist books.

Visit us on the internet:

http://www.grin.com/

http://www.facebook.com/grincom

http://www.twitter.com/grin_com

Beng. Electrical and Electronic Engineering
(Hons.)

EN0624 Individual Engineering Project (2013)

Final Report

Controlling the atmospheric turbulence, microPIC programming

Name – Ninad Gondhalekar

Date of Submission – 21/03/2013

Abstract

Chamber is used to study atmospheric turbulence effects on FSO signals and this experiment is done inside the laboratory to avoid the interference of sunlight light and also it is hard to create turbulence outside laboratory as outside temperature and pressure will affect the turbulence created inside this chamber. This project is all about controlling all parameters (temperature, pressure, humidity) using sensors, fans, thermistors through embedded circuit.

As observed from previous work, high end microPIC (PIC18 series) although it has many functionality and large program memory size, it is hard to control all sensors, fans, thermistor using 1 PIC1866K80, So in this project mid-range PIC (PIC16 series) are used to control sensors, fans and thermistors.

In this project, temperature, humidity, pressure sensors are controlled by different microcontrollers and taking their reading to manage the performance of PWM fans and thermistors inside the chamber. These components are very important to configure and monitor the atmospheric condition inside the chamber.

This project focuses on the use of PIC16 family microcontrollers to be programmed in C language or in assembly to control all sensors, fans and thermistor and build PCB layout.

In this project, Rs-232 or Com port will be used as an interface to control the PIC16 microcontroller instruction and procedure through computer.

Acknowledgement

I want to express my sincere gratitude for their academic assistance and scientific attitude during the procedure of my dissertation.

I would like to thanks my supervisor Dr Michael Elsdon for his positive attitude toward me and encouragement and throughout my project his knowledge and guidance help me in all stages to accomplishment the project.

I also like to thank my second supervisor Dr Joaquin Perez Soler for his warm-hearted help to overcome the difficulty I met throughout the project and helping me in designing critical parts of my project. Special thanks should be voiced to my friends for their patient and help.

Contents

List of Diagrams

Introduction

Northumbria University has research group called Northumbria Communication Research group which is focused on fibre optical communication systems and in free space optical (FSO) communications from laser transmission links to visible light communication. In 2011, in order to reproduce weather conditions from fog to turbulence, this group built an indoor atmospheric chamber and has work extraordinary on the characterization of the FSO links and the effects of weather conditions on them [8]. The suitable atmospheric condition was created by controlling temperature, humidity, pressure sensor, PWM fans and thermistor through PIC18 family series microcontroller. Even top research journals and books have recognized their work in this area. Now, this group is upgrading their facilities which imply an update on the control of the variable like temperature, humidity, pressure, wind speed in the chamber that affects the atmospheric condition replication. They used PIC18 microcontroller (PIC18F66K80) before which belongs to high end. [1] [31]

Previous Work

In previous Project which was based on effects of the sand storm on Free space optical communication, mikroC complier software was used instead of MPLAB software because Mikroc has inbuilt library to set up functionality of microPIC. [1]. In this Project no linear relation between values of register (related to PWM) and wind speed delivered by the fans was found. Measurement of wind speed was done by anemometer EA-3010. MAX32323 component was used to give command to PIC and display the data received from sensors on computer. To set up UART mikroC was used as it contains lots of libraries on UART. Communication of PIC with Pc was set up using software called PuTTY (HyperTerminal can be alternative for PuTTY). For temperature measurement DS18B20 sensor is used which is digital sensor which is one-wire bus device. For pressure measurement, MPX4115A is used

7

which is analogue and ADC converter which available in PIC18 series. For Humidity Measurement, SHT11 is used which is digital sensor which can measure both temperature and humidity but here it's used only for humidity. In this project, 5 out of 10 fans couldn't control with PWM (pulse width modulation) mode pin of microPIC because DS18B20 and SHT11 need some time to receive and transmit data and if program interrupt these data frame even for some milliseconds, data could misread or PIC will send wrong commands to sensors. At least one timer is needed to generated PWM, which would go often in interrupt function and will mess up other module functioning. The PCB is built around one PIC18f66K80 which limits the number port available for sensors that means numbers of sensors cannot be increased as each humidity sensor needs 2 ports, pressure sensor needs 1 analogue pin for each sensor. [31]

Motivation

Chamber will be used to study atmospheric turbulence effects on FSO signals and this experiment is done inside the laboratory to avoid the interference of sunlight and also it is hard to create turbulence outside laboratory, as outside temperature and pressure will affect the turbulence created inside this chamber. This project is all about controlling all parameters (temperature, pressure, humidity) using sensors, fans, thermistors through embedded circuit. As observed from previous work, high end microPIC (PIC18 series) although it has many functionality and large program memory size, it is hard to control all sensors, fans, thermistor using 1 PIC1866K80, So in this project mid-range PIC (PIC16 series) are used to control sensors, fans and thermistors.[1] [31]

Literature review

Free Space Optical Communication

Free space optical communication (FSO) is an optical communication technology which transmits data for telecommunications or computer networking by propagating light in form of laser using lenses and mirrors to focus and redirect the beam through free space (e.g. Air, outer space, vacuum).[31]

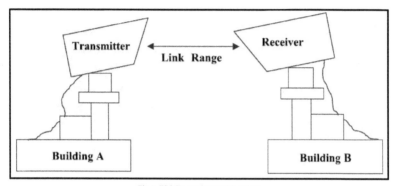

Fig 1: FSO Transmitter and Receiver

Other name for FSO communication is Wireless Optical communication (WOC), fibreless or Laser Communication .Nowadays, it has witness a vast development and is categorised among as one of the different types of wireless communication. At clear atmospheric conditions, it provides a wide service and requires point-to-point connection between transmitter and receiver FSO is basically the same as fiber optic transmission. The difference is that the laser beam is collimated and sent through atmosphere from the transmitter, rather than guided through optical fiber [2]. The FSO technique uses modulated laser beam to transfer carrying data from a transmitter to a receiver. FSO is affected by attenuation of the atmosphere due to the instable weather conditions. Since the atmosphere channel, through which light propagates is not ideal.[28] [29]

FSO systems are sensitive to bad weather conditions such as fog, haze, dust, rain and turbulence. All of these conditions act to attenuate light and could block the light path in the atmosphere. As a result of these challenges, we have to study weather conditions in detail before installing FSO systems. This is to reduce effects of the atmosphere also to ensure that the transmitted power is sufficient and minimal losses during bad weather.

Advantages and Disadvantages of FSO

The free space optics advantages and disadvantages are worth exploration. After all, whenever a new method of modern communication is developed it is important to consider all the positives and negatives that come along with it.

There are many advantages of free space optics. Such as, lower costs associated with the system, no fiber optic cables to lay, no expensive rooftop installations required and no security upgrades necessary, the system upgrades are generally made quite easily and no RF license is needed.[23] Another advantage of free space optical communication is that it is incredibly fast. Currently, these systems can transmit a large amount of data, 1.25 GB per second [30] [27]. In fact, in future it is expected to increase to a whopping 10 GB per second. This speed is because of the fact that the signals can be transmitted through the air faster than they can be transmitted through fiber optic cables. The signals are sent from one wireless unit to another in a direct line through the atmosphere. Another advantage of free space optics is that the radio frequencies don't interference with the signal . This means fewer disruptions to the information flow [22].

There are also a number of drawbacks of FSO. Free space optical communication is subject to atmospheric disturbances and conditions. Thick fog is one of the most problematic forms of interference for wireless optical communication [25]. This is because the moisture in the fog can reflect, absorb, and scatter the signal. Absorption and scattering can both occur whenever there is a lot of moisture in the air. Absorption of the signal causes a decrease in signal strength. Scattering does not cause a decrease in signal strength, but rather causes the signal to be sent off in different directions. This is an issue particularly over long distances. Physical obstructions can also be a problem [26]. These are generally temporary and include birds, cranes, and even building sway that results from earthquakes. Scintillation, which is heat rising from the earth or something man-made, can also disrupt the signal. There have also been concerns about the level of safety of free space optical communication due to the use of lasers. This is of concern particularly when it comes to eye safety and to the high voltages required to power the systems. However, there have been strict regulations put into effect to minimize the risks.

Overall, FSO has got many advantages than its disadvantages. To have a reliable and less expensive method of wireless communication is of the utmost importance in today's mobile society and free space optics makes this possible. All advantages and disadvantages of free space optical communication are given below.

ADVANTAGES	DISADVANTAGES
No need of spectrum license	Beam dispersion
It is full duplex	Atmospheric absorption (Rain, Snow, pollution)
More secure due to narrowness and high directionality compared to RF and other wireless system	Interference due to back ground sources like (sunlight, etc.)
Easy to install	Scintillation effect
Fresnel zone is not require	Mie – scattering effect
Protocol transparency	Rayleigh scattering effect
High bit rates	Shadowing
Low bit error ration over short distance	Pointing stability in wind
No optical fibre is required	Temporary blocking of signal due physical obstruction like bird, etc

FSO System

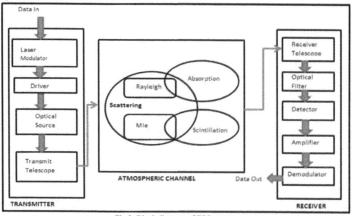

Fig 2: Block diagram of FSO system

FSO communication is a line of sight technology that uses laser beam for sending the very high bandwidth digital data from one point to another through atmosphere. This can be achieved by using a modulated narrow laser beam lunched from a transmission station to transmit it through atmosphere and subsequently received at the receiver station. The generalized FSO system is illustrated in Fig. (2), it is typically consists of transmitter, FSO channel and a receiver.

11

a. Transmitter

Transmitter transforms the electrical signal to an optical signal and it modulates the laser beam to transfer carrying data to the receiver through the atmosphere channel. The transmitter consists of four parts as shown in Fig. (2): laser modulator, driver, optical source and transmit telescope.

Laser modulator

Laser modulation means the data were carried by a laser beam. The modulation technique can be implemented in following two common methods: internal modulation and external modulation [2].

Internal modulation: is a process which occurs inside the laser resonator and it depends on the change caused by the additive components and change the intensity of the laser beam according to the information signal.

External modulation: is the process which occurs outside the laser resonator and it depends on both the polarization phenomena and the refractive dualism phenomenon.

Driver

Driver circuit of a transmitter transforms an electrical signal to an optical signal by varying the current flow through the light source.

Optical source

Optical source may be a laser diode (LD) [21] or light emitting diode (LED), which used to convert the electrical signal to optical signal.

A laser diode is a device that produces optical radiation by the process of stimulated emission photons from atoms or molecules of a lasing medium, which have been excited from a ground state to a higher energy level. A laser diode emits light that is highly monochromatic and very directional. This means that the LD's output has a narrow spectral width and small output beam angle divergence. LDs produce light waves with a fixedphase relationship between points on the electromagnetic wave. There are two common types of laser diode: Nd:YAG solid state laser and fabry-perot and distributed-feedback laser (FP and DFB) [3].

Laser source selection criteria for FSO

The selection of a laser source for FSO applications depends on various factors. They factors can be used to select an appropriate source for a particular application. To understand the descriptions of the source performance for a specific application, one should understand these detector factors. Typically the factors that impact the use of a specific light source include the following [4]:

- Price and availability of commercial components
- Transmission power and lifetime
- Modulation capabilities
- Eye safety
- Physical dimensions and compatibility with other transmission media.

Transmitter telescope

The transmitter telescope collects, collimates and directs the optical radiation towards the receiver telescope at the other end of the channel.

b. FSO channel

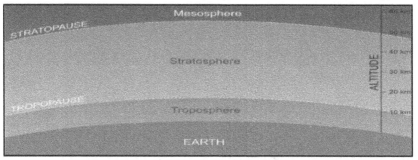

Fig 3: Atmosphere layers of earth

For FSO links, the propagation medium is the atmosphere. The atmosphere may be regarded as series of concentric gas layers around the earth. Three principal atmospheric layers are defined in the homosphere [5], the troposphere, stratosphere and mesosphere. These layers are differentiated by their temperature gradient with respect to the altitude. In FSO communication, we are especially interested in the troposphere because this is where most weather phenomena occur and FSO links operate at the lower part of this layer [5].

The atmosphere is primarily composed of nitrogen (N_2, 78%), oxygen (O_2, 21%), and argon (Ar, 1%), but there are also a number of other elements, such as water (H_2O, 0 to 7%) and carbon dioxide (CO_2, 0.01 to 0.1%), present in smaller amounts. There are also small particles that contribute to the composition of the atmosphere; these include particles (aerosols) such as haze, fog, dust, and soil [6][20].

Propagation characteristics of FSO through atmosphere drastically change due to communication environment, especially, the effect of weather condition is strong. The received signal power fluctuates and attenuates by the atmospheric obstacles such as rain, fog, haze and turbulence in the propagation channel [22] . The atmospheric attenuation

13

results from the interaction of the laser beam with air molecules and aerosols along the propagation. The main effects on optical wireless communication are absorption, scattering, and scintillation [7].

c. Receiver

The receiver optics consists of five parts as shown in Fig. 2: receiver telescope, optical filter, detector, amplifier and demodulator.[19]

Receiver telescope

The receiver telescope collects and focuses the incoming optical radiation on to the photo detector. It should be noted that a large receiver telescope aperture is desirable because it collects multiple uncorrelated radiation and focuses their average on the photo detector [8].

Optical filter

By introducing optical filters that allow mainly energy at the wavelength of interest to impinge on the detector and reject energy at unwanted wavelengths, the effect of solar illumination can be significantly minimized [6].

Detector

The detector also called photodiode (PD) is a semiconductor devices which converts the photon energy of light into an electrical signal by releasing and accelerating current conducting carriers within the semiconductors. Photodiodes operate based on photoconductivity principals, which is an enhancement of the conductivity of p-n semiconductor junctions due to the absorption of electromagnetic radiation. The diodes are generally reverse-biased and capacitive charged [9]. The two most commonly used photodiodes are the pin photodiode and the avalanche photodiode (APD) because they have good quantum efficiency and are made of semiconductors that are widely available commercially [10].

Features of detector

The performance characteristics indicate how a detector responds to an input of light energy. They can be used to select an appropriate detector for a particular application. To understand the descriptions of detector performance and to be able to pick a detector for a specific application, one should understand these detector characteristics. In general, the following properties are needed [18]:

- A high response at the wavelength to be detected.

- A small value for the additional noise is introduced by the detector.

- Sufficient speed of response.

14

Effects of Atmospheric Attenuation of FSO Communication

Clear air turbulence phenomena affect the propagation of optical beam by both spatial and temporal random fluctuations of refractive index due to temperature, pressure, and wind variations along the optical propagation path [11][12]. Atmospheric turbulence primary causes phase shifts of the propagating optical signals resulting in distortions in the wave front. These distortions, referred to as optical aberrations, also cause intensity distortions, referred to as scintillation. Moisture, aerosols, temperature and pressure changes produce refractive index variations in the air by causing random variations in density [13]. These variations are referred to as eddies and have a lens effect on light passing through them. When a plane wave passes through these eddies, parts of it are refracted randomly causing a distorted wave front with the combined effects of variation of intensity across the wave front and warping of the isophase surface [14]. The refractive index can be described by the following relationship [15] [20]:

$$n - 1 \approx 79 \times \frac{P}{T}$$

Where:

P is the atmospheric pressure in [mbar].

T is the temperature in Kelvin [K].

If the size of the turbulence eddies are larger than the beam diameter, the whole laser beam bends. If the sizes of the turbulence eddies are smaller than the beam diameter the laser beam bends partially, they become distorted. Small variations in the arrival time of various components of the beam wave front produce constructive and destructive interference and result in temporal fluctuations in the laser beam intensity at the receiver.

Refractive index structure

Refractive index structure parameter C_n^2 is the most significant parameter that determines the turbulence strength. Clearly, C_n^2 depends on the geographical location, altitude, and time of day. Close to ground, there is the largest gradient of temperature associated with the largest values of atmospheric pressure (and air density). Therefore, one should expect larger values C_n^2 at sea level. As the altitude increases, the temperature gradient decreases and so the air density with the result of smaller values of C_n^2 [3].

In applications that envision a horizontal path even over a reasonably long distance, one can assume C_n^2 to be practically constant. Typical value of C_n^2 for a weak turbulence at ground level can be as little as $10^{-17} m^{-2/3}$, while for a strong turbulence it can be up to $10^{-13} m^{-2/3}$ or larger. However, a number of parametric models have been formulated to describe the C_n^2 profile and among those, one of the more used models is the Hufnagel-Valley [16] given by Eq.

$$C_n^2(h) = 0.00594(v/27)^2 \times (10^{-5}h)^{10} \exp(-h/1000) + 2.7 \times 10^{-16} \exp(-h/1500) + A_0 \exp(-h/100)$$

Where:

h is the altitude in [m].

v is the wind speed at high altitude [m/s].

A_0 is the turbulence strength at the ground level, $A_0 = 1.7 \times 10^{-14} m^{-2/3}$.

The most important variable in its change is the wind and altitude. Turbulence has three main effects [36]; scintillation, beam wander and beam spreading.

Scintillation

Scintillation may be the most noticeable one for FSO systems [9]. Light traveling through scintillation will experience intensity fluctuations, even over relatively short propagation paths. The scintillation index, σ_i2 describes such intensity fluctuation as the normalized variance of the intensity fluctuations given by Eq. (19) [3]:

$$\sigma_i^2 = \frac{<(I-<I>)^2>}{<I>^2} = \frac{<I^2>}{<I>^2} - 1$$

Where:

$I = |E|^2$: is the signal irradiance (or intensity).

The strength of scintillation can be measured in terms of the variance of the beam amplitude or irradiance σ_i given by the following:

$$\sigma_i^2 = 1.23 \, C_n^2 k^{7/6} L^{11/6} \qquad \text{----}(20)$$

Here, $k = 2\pi/\lambda$ is the wave number and this expression suggests that longer wavelengths experience a smaller variance.

Where the Eq. (20) is valid for the condition of weak turbulence mathematically corresponding to $\sigma_i^2 < 1$. Expressions of lognormal field amplitude variance depend on: the nature of the electromagnetic wave traveling in the turbulence and on the link geometry [3].

Performances of FSO Links

There are many parameters to analysis the performance of FSO links like bit error ratio (BER), received power, geometrical loss, and link margin. According to theory, the basic principal of communication states that received power must be less than transmitted power, $P_R \leq P_T$ [10].

$P_R = P_T - $ Total Losses

Here P_R is received power and P_T is transmitted power and units are dBm. Losses of transmitted signal in FSO system are atmospheric phenomena (L_{atm} (dB)), geometrical loss (L_{geo} (dB)) and system loss (L_{sys} (dB)). Geometrical and system loss (define by manufacturer) occur inside FSO transceiver and fixed which cannot be neglected. Geometrical loss is calculated by

$$L_{geo} = -10 \log \left[\frac{4A}{\prod(l\emptyset)^2}\right]$$

Here l (km) is the distance of optical path of laser beam, $\emptyset$ (mrad) is the divergence angle which is cone angle emitted light from transmitter and A (m^2) is the total area of receiver apertures on FSO unit. Atmospheric loss for any laser power is given by Beers-Lambert Law [11].

$$L_{atm} = e^{-\mathcal{O}l}$$

Here $\mathcal{O}$ is typical attenuation coefficient (0.1 for clear air) and l (km) is transmittance range. Bit error ratio (BER) is ratio of the number of errors to total number of bits.

$$BER = \frac{ne}{Nb}$$

Here ne is number of received error bits and Nb is the number of all transmitted bits for long period. [17]

Aim and Objectives

In this project, the aim is to control temperature, humidity, pressure sensors by different microcontrollers and taking their reading to manage the performance of PWM fans and thermistors inside the chamber. These components are very important to configure and monitor the atmospheric condition inside the chamber. This atmospheric condition which is created in chamber will be used to see how real atmospheric turbulence affects the free space optical signal. The Rs-232 or Com port will be used as an interface to control the PIC16 microcontroller instruction and procedure through computer. For temperature measurement, DS18B20 digital sensors will be used, for humidity measurement, SHT11 digital sensors will be used and for pressure measurement, MPX4115a analogue sensor will be used.

1. Programming microPIC for temperature measurement

The first objective is to do research on working of DS18B20 temperature sensors, after that select suitable mid-range microPIC (PIC16 micro controller). While selecting microPIC process, microPIC should be selected which has sufficient memory size, has internal oscillator to reduce PCB size, which can programmed with In-circuit serial programmer (PICKIT 2 or PICKIT 3) has USART feature in it. After selecting microPIC, this microPIc should be programmed using C language or assembly language. Then PCB for temperature sensor should made using software like Proteus or Eagle.

2. Programming microPIC for humidity measurement

The second objective is to do research on working of SHT11 humidity sensor, followed by selecting suitable mid-range microPIC (PIC16 micro controller). While selecting microPIC process, microPIC should be selected which has sufficient memory size, has internal oscillator to reduce PCB size, which supports In-circuit serial programming (ICSP) so that it can be programmed with PICKIT 3 and has USART feature in it. After selecting microPIC, this microPIC should be programmed using C language or assembly language. Then PCB for temperature sensor should made using software like Proteus or Eagle.

3. Programming microPIC for pressure measurement

Similarly, third objective is to do research on working of MPX4115a pressure sensor, followed by selecting suitable mid-range microPIC (PIC16 micro controller). While selecting microPIC process, microPIC should be selected which has sufficient memory size, has internal oscillator to reduce PCB size, has internal analogue to digital converter, supports In-circuit serial programming (ICSP) so that it can be programmed with PICKIT 3 and has USART feature in it. After selecting microPIC, this microPIC should be programmed using C language or assembly language. Then PCB for temperature sensor should made using software like Proteus or Eagle.

4. Programming microPIC for controlling PWM fan

Fourth objective is to do research on working of 12 Volts DC PWM fan, followed by selecting suitable mid-range microPIC (PIC16 micro controller). While selecting microPIC process, microPIC should be selected which has sufficient memory size, has internal oscillator to reduce PCB size, has Pulse width modulating feature, supports In-circuit serial programming (ICSP) so that it can be programmed with PICKIT 3 and has USART feature in it. After selecting microPIC, this microPIC should be programmed using C language or assembly language. Then PCB for temperature sensor should made using software like Proteus or Eagle.

5. Programming microPIC for controlling Thermistors

Fifth and last objective is to do research on working of thermistor with microcontroller, followed by selecting suitable mid-range microPIC (PIC16 micro controller). While selecting microPIC process, microPIC should be selected which has sufficient memory size, has internal oscillator to reduce PCB size, supports In-circuit serial programming (ICSP) so that it can be programmed with PICKIT 3 and has USART feature in it. After selecting microPIC, this microPIC should be programmed using C language or assembly language. Then PCB for temperature sensor should made using software like Proteus or Eagle

Temperature Sensors

Working of DS18B20 temperature sensor

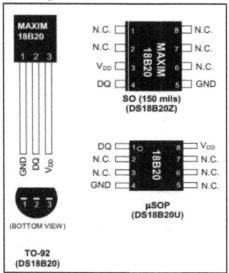

Fig 4: Pin diagram of DS18B20

In the project DS18B20 temperature sensor (TO-92) is used whose pin diagram is shown in Fig4. This temperature sensor measure temperature and convert it in digital format before sending to master device on one-wire bus. This sensor provides user-configurable resolution of 9,10, 11 and 12 bits which relates to increments by 0.5^0 C, 0.25^0C, 0.125^0C and 0.0625^0C in temperature respectively and its default resolution is 12 bits at power-up. In order to make temperature in Fahrenheit application, a lookup table or conversion sub-function should be include while making program for micro PIC. The output temperature data of DS18B20 is stored as 16bit sign-extended 2's complement number in its temperature register. In temperature register, bit 12 - bit 15 are sign bits (S) and if the temperature is positive then S is equal to 0 and if it is negative then S is equal 1. In Temperature register, bit 0- bit3 represents decimal part of temperature reading, so if resolution is set to 9 bits then bit 0- bit 2 are undefined, if resolution is set to 10 then bit 0 and bit 1 is undefined, if resolution is set to 11 then bit 0 is undefined and if resolution to 12 then bit 0 – bit 3 contain valid data. Fig 6 and Fig 7 shown below gives good idea of temperature and data relationship when DS18B20 is set to resolution of 12.

	BIT 7	BIT 6	BIT 5	BIT 4	BIT 3	BIT 2	BIT 1	BIT 0
LS BYTE	2^3	2^2	2^1	2^0	2^{-1}	2^{-2}	2^{-3}	2^{-4}

	BIT 15	BIT 14	BIT 13	BIT 12	BIT 11	BIT 10	BIT 9	BIT 8
MS BYTE	S	S	S	S	S	2^6	2^5	2^4

S = SIGN

Fig 5: Temperature register of DS18B20

TEMPERATURE (°C)	DIGITAL OUTPUT (BINARY)	DIGITAL OUTPUT (HEX)
+125	0000 0111 1101 0000	07D0h
+85*	0000 0101 0101 0000	0550h
+25.0625	0000 0001 1001 0001	0191h
+10.125	0000 0000 1010 0010	00A2h
+0.5	0000 0000 0000 1000	0008h
0	0000 0000 0000 0000	0000h
-0.5	1111 1111 1111 1000	FFF8h
-10.125	1111 1111 0101 1110	FF5Eh
-25.0625	1111 1110 0110 1111	FE6Fh
-55	1111 1100 1001 0000	FC90h

*The power-on reset value of the temperature register is +85°C.

Fig 6: Temperature and Digital Output of DS18B20 relationship

Power supply for DS18B20

This device can be provided power supply either by an external supply through Vdd pin on device or by parasite power mode, in which this device steals power from one-wire bus through data pin when one-wire bus is held high by master device. By stealing power from one-wire bus some charge is stored on parasite power capacitor in parasite-power control circuitry inside this device which provides power when bus is low. In parasite mode Vdd pin of device is connect to ground as power is taken one-wire bus. For application which need remote temperature reading or in application that are space constrained, this mode is very useful. While performing temperature conversion in parasite mode, master device should provide strong pull-up on one-wire bus and this is achieved by using MOSFET. While the pull-up is enabled, no other activity can take place. This type of power mode is not recommended for measuring temperature above 100^{0}C. Fig 8 shows connection of parasite mode and external power supply mode.

For external power supply mode Vdd pin is connected external power supply, there is no need of MOSFET pullup and master can send or receive data from other devices on the bus while some of them are performing temperature conversion.

Master device on one-wire bus can also determine whether DS18B20 is connected to parasite mode or external power supply mode by issuing Skip ROM command (CCh) followed Read power supply function command (B4h) followed by read time slot which explained in detail DS18B20 Sequence section.

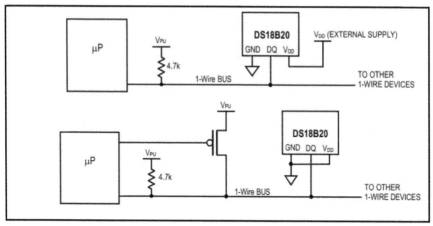

Fig 7: External power supply and parasite mode connection of DS18B20

Memory of DS18B20

Fig 9 shown below shows organisation of DS18B20's memory which consists of SRAM scratchpad with non-volatile EEPROM storage which used to store values of high and low alarm trigger register(T_H and T_L) and configuration register if we want this values not to be lost when power goes off. When this device is powered up, it automatically transfers data

21

from its EEPROM to its Scratchpad byte2, 3 and 4 which is its high and low alarm trigger register and configuration register respectively. When DS18B20 alarm function is not used, then high and low alarm trigger register acts general purpose register.

Byte 0 – byte 1 in scratchpad contain the LSB and MSB of the temperature register. In this register, result of temperature conversation is stored by the device and this register is read-only register. Byte2 – byte 3 are high and low alarm trigger register. From byte 5 to byte 7 are reserved register and cannot be overwritten. read-only Byte number 8 is register which contains the CRC code for bytes 0 to 7 of the scratchpad.

Byte 4 of scratch pad is configuration register. This register is controls the resolution of resulting temperature data from temperature conversion process which is user-configurable. Bit 5 and bit 6 of configuration register are R1 and R0 respectively. If both R0 and R1 are zero then resolution is 9 bits, if R0 is 1 and R1 is 0 then resolution is 10 bits, if R0 is 0 and R1 is 1 then resolution is 11 bits, and if both R0 and R1 are 1 then resolution is 12 bits. There is trade-off between maximum conversion time needed for temperature conversion process and resolution of resulting temperature data. For 9 bits maximum conversion time is 93.75 milliseconds, for 10 bits maximum conversion time is 187.5 milliseconds, for 11 bits maximum conversion time is 375 milliseconds and for 12bits maximum conversation time is 750 milliseconds.

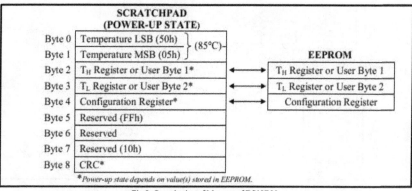

Fig 8: Organisation of Memory of DS18B20

DS18B20 Sequence

Every time to access DS18b20, it important to follow transaction sequence and if this sequence is not followed the sensor will not respond.

- Initialization

- ROM Command
- DS18B20 function command

Initialization

All one-wire transaction begins with initialization sequence. It consists of reset pulse during which bus master goes in transmits mode (Tx) and pulls the one-wire bus low for a minimum of 480 micro-second and after that master release the bus and goes in receive mode (Rx). When bus released, it goes high due to 4.7KΩ pull-up resistor. If there is DS18B20 temperature sensor on one-wire bus, it will detect the rising edge, and it will wait for 15 – 60 micro-seconds and then pulls the one-wire low for 60 - 240 micro-second to transmit presence pulse to master.

ROM Commands

There are five ROM commands each 8 bits long, available for master and it must be send before issuing appropriate DS18B20 function command. ROM commands are important for master on bus to identify specific device out of other devices available on one-wire bus and sent it DS18b20 function command and it is possible to do this as every one-wire sensors has it unique 64 bits ROM code, so master sends that 64bit ROM code and the sensor whose 64bit ROM code matches with it, response to master by sending presence pulse and other devices on bus goes in sleep mode. By ROM commands, master can also determine what types and number of device are present on the one-wire bus.

- Search ROM command (0Fh)

    When system is turned on, in order to find how many and what types of device are present on bus, master must issue search ROM command followed by data exchange between master and slave device on bus, to determine the ROM codes of all devices. The ROM code of all devices is identified by elimination process in which master repeats search ROM cycles till all devices are identified. But if there is only one device is present on bus then instead of Search ROM command, Read ROM command can be issued.

- Read ROM command (33h)

    This command can only be used if there is one device on bus. By this command master reads the ROM code of device. If master send this command when there are more than one device on bus, then there would be data collision as all devices will try to respond at same time.

- Match ROM command (55h)

  If ROM code of all devices is known and master device want to send DS18B20 function command to specific device, then master can issue this command followed by 64-bits ROM code sequence by doing this, slave device whose ROM code matches with the 64 bits ROM code sent by master will respond to function command issued by master device and all other device will wait for reset pulse.

- Skip ROM command (CCh)

  If master wants to address all devices on the bus simultaneously, then this command can be used by master device. For example, master by issuing Skip ROM command followed by Convert T command (given function commands), all DS18B20 device will perform temperature conversion simultaneously.

- Alarm search command (ECh)

  This is command allows master to find whether any DS18B20 device has experienced an alarm condition during recent temperature conversion process. This command works same as Search Rom command.

DS18B20 Function Commands

Function commands are issued by master device to slave devices on bus after ROM command. These commands allow master devices to write, read from DS18B20's scratchpad memory, to start temperature conversion and determine the power supply mode. There are six function commands that master device can issue to slave devices on bus to perform required task.

- Convert T function command (44h)

  By sussing this command by master device, all or specific DS18B20 device on bus will start single temperature conversion and the resulting data gets stored in the 2 byte temperature register in scratchpad memory and the DS18B20 device return to its low-power idle state. When DS18B20 device is powered by external supply, DS18B20 device will respond by transmitting a 0 during temperature conversion process and 1 after finishing this process, if master issue read time slots after Convert T command.

- Write Scratchpad function command (4Eh)

Master device can write 3 bytes of data in DS18B20's Scratchpad by issuing this command. The first data byte is written in byte 2 of scratchpad which is T_H register, the second byte is written in byte 3 of scratchpad which is T_L register and third byte is written in byte 4 of scratchpad which configuration register. All three bytes must be written by transmitting least significant bit first before reset pulse or else data may get corrupted.

- Read Scratchpad function command (BEh)

  By issuing this function command, master device can read the content of the scratchpad and in this process transfer of data starts with least significant bit of byte 0 and continues through scratchpad till 9th byte is read. If some part of scratchpad is needed then master can terminate reading at any time by issuing reset.

- Copy Scratchpad function command (48h)

  By issuing this function command, master device can copy contents of scratchpad of DS18B20 (T_H, T_L, configuration register; Bytes2,3 and 4) to its EEPROM.

- Recall E^2 function command (B8h)

  By issuing this command, master set alarm trigger values (T_H and T_L) and configuration data from DS18B20's EEPROM to DS18b20's Scratchpad bytes 2, 3 and 4 respectively. To determine the status of recall function process master device can issue read time slot after issuing recall function command and during recall process DS18B20 device will transmit 0 and after finishing this process it will transmit 1. Master device can issue this command to DS18B20 device on bus at power-up, to make valid data available in scratchpad when power is applied to slave device.

- Read Power Supply function command

  As DS18B20 device can be powered in two ways i.e. in parasite mode and in external supply mode. Master device can identify whether device is connect to power supply in parasite mode or in external supply mode by issuing this command. If master device issue read time slot after issuing read power supply function command, DS18B20 will pull the bus low if it connected in parasite mode and will let the bus remain high if DS18B20 is connected to external power supply.

Coding for PIC16F627A and DS18B20 in C language

This coding in C language has been done in MikroC software ad this software has all needed library in-buit. This program has been made according to data given in datasheet of DS18B20 sensor. In this program, only one sensor was tested to check whether sensor is responding to program or not. After completing this objective, next objective was to make program for more than 1 sensor.

```c
/* program name: PIC16F627A and DS18B20
   Description: Program made to get reading from single
                DS18B20 Sensor and display value on PC
                through USART
   Configuration: Microcontroller – PIC16F627A
                  Oscillator – Internal , 4Mhz */

/* Address of the DS18B20*/
char ROMCODE[8] = {0x28, 0xF1, 0xFB, 0xAB, 3, 0, 0, 0x99};

const unsigned short TEMP_RESOLUTION = 12;
char retour[] = {0,0,0,0};
char *text = "000.0000";
unsigned temp;

/* List of different functions */
void Display_Temperature(unsigned int temp2write);
char OneWire_Reset();
void OneWire_Write_Byte(unsigned char data_byte);
void OneWire_Write_Bit(unsigned char data_bit);
unsigned char OneWire_Read_Byte();
char OneWire_Read_Bit();
int OneWire_Search_ROM();
int rom_byte(int id_bit_number);
void OneWire_ROM(char *address);

void main(){
 while(1){
 OneWire_Reset();
 OneWire_Write_Byte(0xCC); // Skip ROM
 OneWire_Write_Byte(0x44); // Convert T
 Delay_ms(1000);
 OneWire_Reset();
 OneWire_Write_Byte(0x55); // MATCH ROM
 OneWire_ROM(ROMCODE); // calling first device
 OneWire_Write_Byte(0xBE); // read scratch pad
 temp = 0;
 temp = OneWire_Read_Byte();
 temp =(OneWire_Read_Byte() << 8)+temp;

 WordToHex(temp,retour);

 UART2_Write_Text("Temperature : ");
 Display_temperature(temp);
```

```
UART2_Write_Text(" ");
}}

void OneWire_ROM(char *address){
 int i;
 for(i=0;i<8;i++)
 {
   OneWire_Write_Byte(*address);
   *address++;
}}

/* MikroC code was used for the conversion to celsius temperature */
void Display_Temperature(unsigned int temp2write) {
 const unsigned short RES_SHIFT = TEMP_RESOLUTION - 8;
 char temp_whole;
 unsigned int temp_fraction;
 // Check if temperature is negative
 if (temp2write & 0x8000) {
   text[0] = '-';
   temp2write = ~temp2write + 1;
   }
 // Extract temp_whole
 temp_whole = temp2write >> RES_SHIFT ;
 // Convert temp_whole to characters
 if (temp_whole/100)
   text[0] = temp_whole/100  + 48;
 else
   text[0] = '0';
  // Extract tens digit
 text[1] = (temp_whole/10)%10 + 48;
 // Extract ones digit
 text[2] = temp_whole%10   + 48;
 // Extract temp_fraction and convert it to unsigned int
 temp_fraction  = temp2write << (4-RES_SHIFT);
 temp_fraction &= 0x000F;
 temp_fraction *= 625;
 // Convert temp_fraction to characters
 text[4] = temp_fraction/1000   + 48; // Extract thousands digit
 text[5] = (temp_fraction/100)%10 + 48; // Extract hundreds digit
 text[6] = (temp_fraction/10)%10  + 48; // Extract tens digit
 text[7] = temp_fraction%10    + 48; // Extract ones digit
 // Print temperature with UART
 UART2_Write_Text(" ");
 UART2_Write_Text(text);
}

unsigned char OneWire_Reset()
{
```

```c
unsigned char resetWire;
TRISB.RB0 = 0; // pre reset settings
LATB.RB0 = 0; // RB4 is low
Delay_us(480); // wait for 480us
// we must release and wait for the response pulse
TRISB.RB0 = 1;
Delay_us(100);
//RB4 should be low, if it's the case,
// then there is a response
resetWire = !PORTB.RB0;
Delay_us(130);
Delay_us(250);
// if RB4 low, that means that devices are present
return resetWire;
}

void OneWire_Write_Byte(unsigned char data_byte){
 int i;
 for(i=0;i<8;i++) // one byte to transmit
 {
  TRISB.RB0 = 0;
  // the master is initiating the writing
  //by pulling the bus low
  LATB.RB0 = 0;
  // The master must release the bus within
  //15us if needed, otherwise it keeps pulling low
  Delay_us(4);
  /* This line of code allow the master to either
   release the bus to write a 1
  or to hold the bus down and write a 0 */
  TRISB.RB0 = data_byte & 0x01;
  // the bus master must hold this state for at least 60us
  Delay_us(60);
  // recovery by releasing the bus
  TRISB.RB0 = 1;
  // minimum of a 1us recovery time between
  //individual write slots, here I gave 6 us
  Delay_us(6);
  // we have to push the bit, because we receive LSB first
  data_byte = data_byte >> 1;
 }}

unsigned char OneWire_Read_Byte(){
 unsigned char data_read = 0x00;
 int i;
 for(i=0;i<8;i++)
 {
  TRISB.RB0 = 0;
```

```
LATB.RB0 = 0;
/*read time slot is initiated by the master
device pulling the 1-Wire bus low for a minimum
of 1us and then releasing the bus    */
Delay_us(2);
TRISB.RB0 = 1;
 /*Therefore, the master must release the bus and
  then sample the bus state within 15us from
  the start of the slot. I chose 8us to make a
  total of 10us which is lower than 15 us*/
 Delay_us(8);

 data_read = (PORTB.RB0 << i) + data_read;
 /*All read time slots must be a minimum of 60us */
 Delay_us(50);
}
return data_read;
}
```

Arduino Program for more than 1 DS18B20 temperature sensors

Since due some reason, program made for PIC was not working. DS18B20 sensor was not responding to reset pulse given by PIC and it was checked in oscilloscope after sending reset pulse by PIC, there was no present pulse sent by DS18B20 sensor. So in order see temperature measurement of DS18B20 sensor, program was made on Arduino. Arduino has all one-wire library in its software which make coding simple compare to PIC coding, moreover there is less wiring required between arduino and DS18B20 temperature sensor. Code for Arduino is given below. Two arduino programs were made, one was to find ROM code of each DS18B20 sensor and another was to read 3 DS18B20 sensors.

First arduino program is to find unqiue ROM code of DS18B20 sensor.

```
// This sketch looks for 1-wire devices and
// prints their addresses (serial number) to
// the UART, in a format that is useful in Arduino sketches

#include <OneWire.h>
OneWire  ds(3); // Connect your 1-wire device to pin 3

void setup(void) {
  Serial.begin(9600);
```

```
  discoverOneWireDevices();}

void discoverOneWireDevices(void) {
  byte i;
  byte present = 0;
  byte data[12];
  byte addr[8];

  Serial.print("Looking for 1-Wire devices...\n\r");
  while(ds.search(addr)) {
   Serial.print("\n\rFound \'1-Wire\' device with address:\n\r");
   for( i = 0; i < 8; i++) {
    Serial.print("0x");
    if (addr[i] < 16) {
     Serial.print('0');
    }
    Serial.print(addr[i], HEX);
    if (i < 7) {
     Serial.print(", ");
    }
   }
   if ( OneWire::crc8( addr, 7) != addr[7]) {
     Serial.print("CRC is not valid!\n");
     return;
   }}
  Serial.print("\n\r\n\rThat's it.\r\n");
  ds.reset_search();
  return;}
void loop(void) {
 // nothing to see here}
```

This second arduino program in which reading from 3 DS18B20 sensors.

```
// This Arduino sketch reads 3 DS18B20 "1-Wire" digital
// temperature sensors.
```

```
#include <OneWire.h>
#include <DallasTemperature.h>

// Data wire is plugged into pin 3 on the Arduino
#define ONE_WIRE_BUS 3

// Setup a oneWire instance to communicate with any OneWire devices
OneWire oneWire(ONE_WIRE_BUS);

// Pass our oneWire reference to Dallas Temperature.
DallasTemperature sensors(&oneWire);


// Assign the addresses of your 1-Wire temp sensors.
DeviceAddress first_Thermometer = { 0x28, 0x75, 0xE6, 0xAF, 0x04, 0x00, 0x00, 0x86 };

DeviceAddress second_Thermometer = { 0x28, 0x2B, 0xF2, 0xAF, 0x04, 0x00, 0x00, 0xD8 };
DeviceAddress third_Thermometer = { 0x28, 0x07, 0x94, 0xB0, 0x04, 0x00, 0x00, 0x3C };

void setup(void){
 // starting serial port
 Serial.begin(9600);
 // Start up the library
 sensors.begin();
 // set the resolution to 10 bit
 sensors.setResolution(first_Thermometer, 10);
 sensors.setResolution(second_Thermometer, 10);
 sensors.setResolution(third_Thermometer, 10);
}

void printTemperature(DeviceAddress deviceAddress){
 float tempC = sensors.getTempC(deviceAddress);
 if (tempC == -127.00) {
  Serial.print("Error getting temperature");}
  else {
  Serial.print("C: ");
  Serial.print(tempC);
  Serial.print(" F: ");
  Serial.print(DallasTemperature::toFahrenheit(tempC));
 }}

void loop(void){
 delay(2000);
 Serial.print("Getting temperatures...\n\r");
 sensors.requestTemperatures();
 Serial.print("1st temperature is: ");
```

```
printTemperature(first_Thermometer);
Serial.print("\n\r");
Serial.print("2nd temperature is: ");
printTemperature(second_Thermometer);
Serial.print("\n\r");
Serial.print("3rd temperature is: ");
printTemperature(third_Thermometer);
Serial.print("\n\r\n\r");
}
```

PCB and schematic diagram

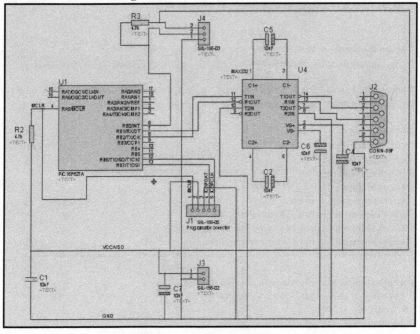

Fig 9: Schematic diagram of DS18B20

Above Schematic is of DS18B20 temperature sensor. PIC16F627A, which shown in schematics as U1 component, is chosen as microPIC for temperature sensor which has 1024 words flash memory, 224 bytes RAM memory, has USART serial communication, has internal oscillator of 4MHz and can be programmed using PICKIT 3. J1 component is 5 head pins which is used to connect PICKIT 3 to program PIC16F627A. The connection between microPIC and J1 are made according to datasheet of PICKIT 3. PIC16F627 can be programmed again and again using PICKIT 3 without taking it out of PCB, if program doesn't work as expected. Component J3 is 2 pin headpins through which constant 5 Vdc and ground can be connected to circuit. Component J4 is 3 pin headpins through which DS18B20 sensors can be connected, pin 1 of J3 is ground pin, pin 2 is one-wire bus which is used for communication between sensors and microPIC and pin 3 of J3 is Vdd pin. Pin 2 and Pin 3 are connected with 4.7K ohms pull-up resistor as suggested in datasheet of DS18B20 sensor. Max3232CPE+ chip is used for communication microPIC with computer which shown as U4 component in schematics and connection around this chip is done according to datasheet of MAX3232CPE+ chip. Component J2 is 9 pin D-type connector which used to connect circuit to computer. PCB diagram shown below is made using schematic shown above.

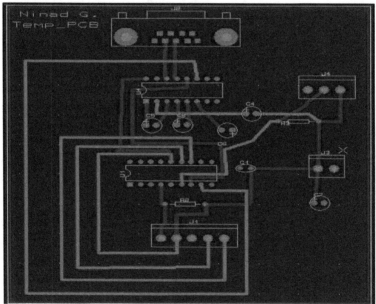

Fig 10: PCB of DS18B20 sensor

Humidity Sensor

Working of SHT11

SHT11 humidity sensor must be supplied with 2.4 – 5.5 Volts. Vdd pin and ground pin of this sensor should be decoupled with 100nF capacitor as shown in Fig 11. I^2C protocol is not addressed by this sensor but can be connected to I^2C bus if there is no interference with other devices which are present on I^2C bus.

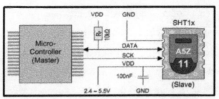

In order to synchronize the communication between microPIC and SHT11, SCK (serial clock input) is used. No minimum SCK frequency is required as interface consists of fully static logic. For sending data from sensor to microPIC and from microPIC to sensor, DATA tri-state pin is used. Data can be sent from microPIC to SHT11 on SCK's raising edge (serial clock input) and should remain stable till SCK (serial clock input) is high and when SCK (serial clock input) goes low, data value can change. For reading data send by sensor, data is valid 200 nano-seconds after SCK (serial clock input) has gone low and remains valid until next falling edge of SCK (serial clock input).

Communicating with SHT11 humidity sensor

When SHT11 is powered up, slew rate should not fall below 1 Volts/ms. SHT11 sensor needs 11ms to get to sleep state after it is power up and during this time microPIC should not send any command. Like DS18B20 temperature sensor, SHT11 sensor needs a transmission start sequence issued by microPIC to start the transmission which is done by lowering the data line while SCK is held high and then putting low pulse on SCK followed by raising DATA again after SCK is high as shown in Fig 12. After transmission start sequence, miicroPIC should send command to SHT11. This command consist of three address bits (which is '000') and followed by five command bits (Fig 13 shown list of commands). Then if SHT11 sensor recognises the command sent by microPIC, it acknowledges microPIC by pulling DATA pin low at falling edge of 8th SCK clock and then releasing DATA pin to high at falling edge of 9th SCK clock. For measuring relative humidity, microPIC should issue 'measure relative humidity command (00101) and must wait for sensor to complete measuring process which takes maximum of 20ms, 80ms and 320ms for 8 bits, 12 bits and 14 bits respectively. This time is also depends on internal oscillator of microPIC. After completing the measuring process, sensor pulls DATA line low and enters Ideal mode. After sensing that sensor has pull DATA line low, microPIC can restart SCK line to read the resulting data stored in sensor's memory. This data is stored in sensor's memory till microPIC reads that data, therefore microPIC can read that data after doing some other tasks. This data consists of two bytes of measurement data and one byte of CRC checksum (which is option) and is transmitted Most significant bit first. MicroPIC must acknowledge each byte by pulling DATA line low. After acknowledgement of CRC data bit, communication between sensor and micropIC terminates and if CRC checksum is not used, micropIC can stop communication by keeping ACK high after measurement data least significant bit. After completing communication sensor goes sleep mode. In case micropIC lost communication with sensor, micropIC can reset the serial interface by toggling SCK nine or more time while keeping DATA line high. The contents in status registor are preserved after resetting. After resetting serial interface, micropIC should send transmission start sequence again followed by next command. The 8bit checksum secures the whole digital transmission by detecting and eliminating wrong data.

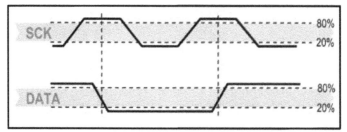

Fig 12: Start the transmission sequence for SHT11

Command	Code
Reserved	0000x
Measure Temperature	**00011**
Measure Relative Humidity	**00101**
Read Status Register	00111
Write Status Register	00110
Reserved	0101x-1110x
Soft reset, resets the interface, clears the status register to default values. Wait minimum 11 ms before next command	**11110**

Fig 13: SHT11 sensor command list

There are some functions available in SHT11 sensor like setting measurement resolution, end-of –battery notification, etc. In applications which demands high speed or extreme low power consumption, then in those case resolution of measurement can be reduce from 12 bits to 8 bits for humidity. If voltage applied to SHT11 sensor goes below 2.45 volts then 6th bit of status register goes low to indicate end-of- battery. The Fig 15 shown below, shows relation between bits in status register of SHT11 sensor and advance function available in SHT11 sensor.

Bit	Type	Description	Default	
7		reserved	0	
6	R	End of Battery (low voltage detection) '0' for VDD > 2.47 '1' for VDD < 2.47	X	No default value, bit is only updated after a measurement
5		reserved	0	
4		reserved	0	
3		For Testing only, do not use	0	
2	R/W	Heater	0	off
1	R/W	no reload from OTP	0	reload
0	R/W	'1' = 8bit RH / 12bit Temp. resolution '0' = 12bit RH / 14bit Temp. resolution	0	12bit RH 14bit Temp.

Fig 14: Status Register of SHT11 sensor

Calculating relative humidity

Following formula should be used to calculate relative humidity to compensate non-linearity of SHT11 and obtain full accuracy.

$$RH_{linear} = C_1 + C_2 \times SO_{RH} + C_3 \times SO_{RH}^2 \ (\% \ RH)$$

SO_{RH}	C_1	C_2	C_3
12 Bits	-2.0468	0.0367	-1.5955e-6
8 Bits	-2.0468	0.5872	-4.0845e-4

Coding for PIC16F627A and SHT11 humidity sensor

This coding in C language has been done in MikroC software. This program has been made according to data given in datasheet of SHT11 sensor.

```
/* program name: PIC16F627A and DS18B20
   Description: Program made to get reading from single
              DS18B20 Sensor and display value on PC
              through USART
   Configuration: Microcontroller – PIC16F627A
                 Oscillator – Internal , 4Mhz */


// PIC16F627A AND SHT11 PROGRAM


// PINS SETTING DEFINATION


#define CLK  PORTB.RB5
```

```
#define DATA PORTB.RB4
#define DATA_X TRISB.RB4

// SHT11 COMMANDS DEFINATION
#define _TEMP  0x03
#define _HUMI  0x05
#define _RESET 0x1E

// CONSTANT DECLARATION
const float d1C = -40.1;
const float d2C = 0.01;
const float C1  = -4.0;
const float C2  = 0.0405;
const float C3  = -0.0000028;

float tempt, humi;
float RH_linear, RH_true;
char txt[15];

// SHT 11 humidity measuring sub-function
unsigned SHT_Measure(char CMD){
  int i;
  unsigned temp = 0;
  char m = 128;
  DATA_X = 0; // PIN linked to data as output
  DATA = 1;   // making data pin high
  CLK = 0;    // making clk pin low

/* resetting the serial interface by
   toggling CLK nine or more time While
   leaving DATA high */
// Connection reset sequence
  for(i=0; i<10; i++)
  {
  CLK = 1;
  CLK = 0;
  }

// Starting Transmission sequence
  DATA = 1;
  CLK  = 1;
  DATA = 0;
  CLK  = 0;
  CLK  = 1;
  DATA = 1;
  CLK  = 0;

//Transmitting  command.
```

```
    for(i=0; i<8; i++)
    {
     if(!(m & CMD)) DATA = 0;
     else DATA = 1;
     CLK = 1;
     CLK = 0;
     m >>= 1; // right justified
    }

    //Checking ACK pulse. return 0 if no ACK pulse.
    DATA_X = 1;
    CLK = 1;
    if(DATA) return 0;
    CLK = 0;
    while(!DATA);

    // wait until data is ready
    while(DATA);

    // get first byte MSB
    for(i=0; i<8; i++)
    {
    temp <<= 1;
    CLK = 1;
    if(DATA) temp |= 1;
    CLK = 0;
    }
    // acknowledge pluse
    DATA_X = 0;
    DATA = 0;
    CLK = 1;
    CLK = 0;
    DATA_X = 1;

    // get second byte  LSB
    for(i=0; i<8; i++)
    {
    temp <<= 1;
    CLK = 1;
    if(DATA) temp |= 1;
    CLK = 0;
    }
    // return value without CRC
    return temp;
}

void main()
{
```

```
// lowing data line
TRISB.RB4 = 0;
// lowing clk line
TRISB.RB5 = 0;
// initialise USART
UART2_Init(9600);
// Setting time for SHT11 after power-up
// as given in data sheet
Delay_ms(11);
//read humidity value from SHT
humi = SHT_Measure(_HUMI);
// time delay for SHT11 to send data to microPIC
Delay_ms(80);
//calculate humidity %RH from value
//formula of RHlinear = C1 + C2*SOrh + C3*SOrh*SOrh  %RH
RH_linear = C1 + (C2*humi);// + (C3*humi*humi);
//formula RHtrue = (Tc-25)*(t1+t2*SOrh)+RHlinear
//convert to string
//floatToStr(RH_true,txt);
floatToStr(RH_linear,txt);
UART2_Write_Text(txt);
UART2_Write_Text(" ");
delay_ms(1000);}
```

Arduino Program for SHT11 sensor

```
#include <SHT1x.h>

// Specify data and clock connections and instantiate SHT1x object
#define dataPin  10
#define clockPin 11
SHT1x sht1x(dataPin, clockPin);

void setup()
{
  Serial.begin(38400); // Open serial connection to report values to host
  Serial.println("Starting up");
}

void loop(){
  float humidity;

  // Read values from the sensor
  humidity = sht1x.readHumidity();

  // Print the values to the serial port
  Serial.print("F. Humidity: ");
```

```
Serial.print(humidity);
Serial.println("%");

delay(2000);}
```

PCB and schematic diagram for SHT11

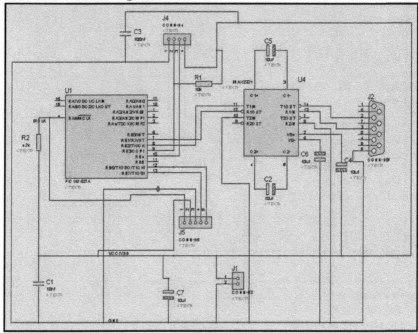

Fig 15: Schematic of SHT11 sensor

Above Schematic is of SHT11 humidity sensor. Like for DS18B20, PIC16F627A, which shown in schematics as U1 component, is chosen as microPIC for humidity sensor which has 1024 words flash memory, 224 bytes RAM memory, has USART serial communication, has internal oscillator of 4MHz and can be programmed using PICKIT 3. J1 component is 5 head pins which is used to connect PICKIT 3 to program PIC16F627A. The connection between microPIC and J1 are made according to datasheet of PICKIT 3. PIC16F627 can be reprogrammed using PICKIT 3 without taking it out of PCB, if program doesn't work as expected. Thus damage to microPIC can be avoided. J1 is 2-pin male-head pins which are connected to stable 5 volt dc and another pin to ground. U4 component is MAX3232CPE+ chip which will connect microPIC to computer through 9-pin D-type connector which is J2 component is schematic. J4 component in schematic is 4-pin male-header pin through SHT11 sensor will be connected and 10K Ohm resistor should be connected between Vdd pin and Data pin and capacitor of 100nF should connected between ground pin and Vdd pin as recommend in datasheet of SHT11 sensor , where pin 1 is ground of SHT11, pin 2 is Serial Data pin of SHT11, pin 3 is Serial Clock pin of SHT11 and pin 4 Vdd pin of SHT11 . Using Schematic of SHT11 sensor PCB board has been made which is shown in Fig 17

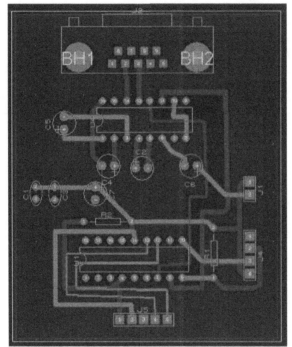

Fig 16: PCB of SHT11 sensor

Pressure Sensor

Working of MPX4115a pressure sensor

MPX4115a pressure sensor is an analogue sensor which needs proper decoupling circuit to interface analogue input of microPIC and output of MPX4115a sensor which is shown in Fig 18 the relation between pressure and sensor output signal is shown in Fig 19

Calculating pressure

The transfer function to calculate pressure (P) is given by

$V_{out} = V_s \times (0.009 \times P - 0.009) \pm$ (Pressure Error $\times$ Temp. Factor $\times 0.009 \times V_s$)

Where $V_s = 5.1 \pm 0.25$ Vdc.

Coding for PIC16F627A and MPX4115a pressure sensor

```
void main()
{
  float input;
  float Voutput;
  char txt[15];
  float Pressure;

  UART2_Init(9600);

  ANCON1.ANSEL10 = 1;

  TRISB.RB0 = 1;

  ADC_Init();
  while(1)
  {

  input = ADC_Read(10);
  Delay_ms(2000);


  Pressure = 0.0271 * input + 10.5;
  FloatToStr(Pressure, txt);
  UART2_Write_Text(" ");
  UART2_Write_Text(txt);
  UART2_Write_Text(" ");
  }
}
```

Arduino Code for MPX4115a

```
// MPX4115a pressure sensor with Arduino program

// KPa to Atm conversion constant
#define kpa2atm 0.00986923267

// pin defination
// MPX4115a output pin is connect to digital pin 0 of arduino
int pressurePin = 0;

// variables
int val;
float pkPa; // pressure in kPa
float pAtm; // pressure in Atm

void setup() {
  Serial.begin(9600);
}

void loop(){
  /* get the pressure */
  val = analogRead(pressurePin);
  pkPa = ((float)val/(float)1023+0.095)/0.009;
  pAtm = kpa2atm*pkPa;

  /* send pressure to serial port */
  Serial.print(pkPa);
  Serial.print("kPa ");
  Serial.print(pAtm);
  Serial.print("Atm ");

  delay(1000);}
```

PCB and Schematic Diagram for MPX4115a pressure sensor

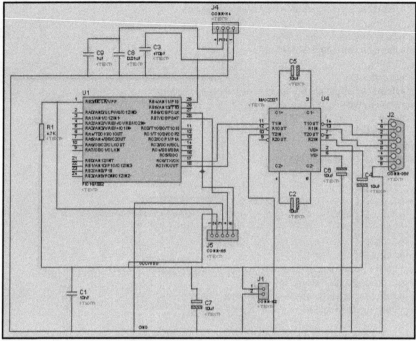

Fig 17: Schematic of MPX4115a Sensor

Above Schematic is of MPX4115a pressure sensor. PIC16F882, which shown in schematics Fig 20 as U1 component, is chosen as microPIC for humidity sensor which has 2048 words flash memory, 128 bytes RAM memory, has USART serial communication, has user configurable internal oscillator of 4MHz and can be programmed using PICKIT 3. J1 component is 5 head pins which is used to connect PICKIT 3 to program PIC16F627A. The connection between microPIC and J1 are made according to datasheet of PICKIT 3. PIC16F627 can be reprogrammed using PICKIT 3 without taking it out of PCB, if program doesn't work as expected. Thus damage to microPIC can be avoided. J1 is 2-pin male-head pins which are connected to stable 5 volt dc and another pin to ground. U4 component is MAX3232CPE+ chip which will connect microPIC to computer through 9-pin D-type connector which is J2 component is schematic. J4 component is 4-pin male-header pin through which MPX4115a pressure sensor will be connected. Proper decoupling is done as given MPX4115a datasheet. Fig 21 shows PCB made for MPX4115a sensor using Schematic of MPX4115a.

44

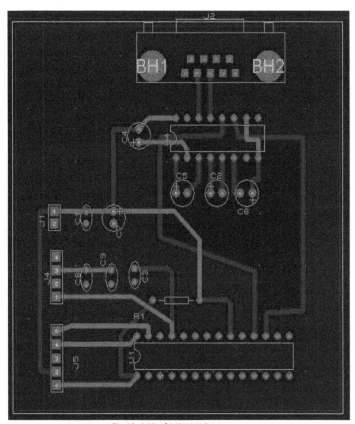

Fig 18: PCB of MPX4115a sensor.

Results and Discussion

Fig 19: ROM Code of 3 DS18B20 sensors

Programs were made for all three sensors in C language for MicroPIC. But since due some reason, sensors were not responding to microPIC, so alternative programs were made on Arduino. Arduino has in-built libraries like one-wire bus library for one-wire devices, sht1X library to support sht1X sensors and has ADC converter inside it, in-built USART and internal oscillator and can be programmed with Arduino software, these features make programming on arduino simpler than programming microPIC. Results for DS18B20 are shown in Fig 19 and Fig 20. As stated before 2 arduino program were made for DS18b20. First program was to find unique 64-bits ROM Code of three DS18B20 sensors (Fig 19) and putting those values in second program temperature reading were obtained (Fig 20). It was observed that all 3 sensors takes little time to show correct measurement when there is sudden change in parameter like temperature In Fig 19, Most significant 8 bits of DS18B20 is it family code which 0x28. Since making program for all three sensors the checking program and remaking it again and then making PCB for these sensors took around 4 months, so research on PWM fans and thermistors couldn't be completed.

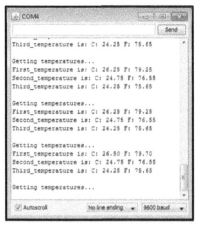

Fig 20: Temperature reading from 3 DS18B20 sensors.

Conclusion

As conclusion of project, Programs were made for PIC but sensors were not responding to microPIC. So program was also made on ardunio to make sensors work. Programming for Fan and thermistor couldn't be completed due to shortage of time.

PCBs for sensors were made and were soldered and simultaneously Programs for PIC 16 were also check but couldn't correct it. It was also tested with oscilloscope no response from sensors was seen on oscilloscope, so there could be problem in protocol of sensors. SHT11 humidity sensor, MPX4115a pressure sensor, and more than one DS18B20 temperature sensors were working fine on arduino and to connect sensors to arduino one breadboard, few resistor and capacitor were used.

47

Appendices

Appendix – A : Costing [31]

- According to salary of newly graduate is £23,132 per year, assuming Graduate work 37 hours per week, the average hourly pay is £12 and 400 hours are needed to complete this project successfully. Therefore graduate cost would be £4800.

- According to salary scale of Northumbria University [16], Dr Eldson's grade is 7.3 therefore yearly salary is £40,139 and Dr Perez's grade is 6.3 therefore yearly salary is £34,555. Both supervise for half an hour per week for 7 months (Oct'11-Apr'12) therefore hour spent on project is 14.

- Lab technician yearly salary at Northumbria University is 22,212, therefore assuming that he works 37 per week hourly wages come upto £11.5.

Name	Yearly salary (£)	Hourly salary (£)	Hours spent	Total Wage (£)
Dr. Elsdon	40,139	21	14	294
Dr. Perez	34,555	18	14	252
Designer (Ninad)	23,132	12	400	4800
Lab technician	22,212	11.5	1	11.5
TOTAL (£)				5,357.5

Table – 2: Labour Resource and Wages

Facilities Resource and Cost [31]

- Northumbria University has provided access to Laboratory to perform experiment where indoor chamber is located. University has also provided all equipment like power supply equipment, computers, etc., related to project, lab technician who will build the PCB for project, book resource and access to website like IEEE*Xplore*, ScienceDirect, etc.

Name of the Book	Cost (£)	Availability
C programming for scientists and engineers	32.29	University Library
C by examples	20.45	University Library
PIC projects: a practical approach	21.99	University Library
The craft of scientific writing	18.69	University Library
The craft of scientific presentation	23.75	University Library
Optical wireless communication: system and channel modelling with MATLAB	72.16	University Library
Wireless optical communication systems	16.79	University Library

Software Resource and Cost

- Various Softwares will be used for doing this project. Three softwares (MPLAB, Source Boost, Mikro C) will be used as C and Assembly complier. Two softwares (ORCAD, EAGLE 6.2.0) will be used for PCB design and proteus 7 professional software will be used to stimulate the circuit. Multimatrix software and hardware will be used to program PIC microcontroller. [31]

Name of Software	Availability
MPLAB	All Labs in E block (Ellison Building)
Source Boost	All Labs in E block (Ellison Building)
Mikro C	Designer laptop
ORCAD	All Labs in E block (Ellison Building)
EAGLE 6.2.0	All Labs in E block (Ellison Building)
Multimatrix	Ellison Building EBE204, EBE206
Proteus 7 Professional	All Labs in E block (Ellison Building)
MATLAB	All Labs in E block (Ellison Building)
PuTTY	All Labs in E block (Ellison Building)
LabView	All Labs in E block (Ellison Building)

Hardware Resource and cost [31]

- Main Component required for project is mention in table 5 with cost and whether the component is provided by University. The cost of component is taken farnell website [17] assuming 10 units are purchased at a time.
- PCB board dimension is 30 x 22 cm and different microPICs are needed to control temperature sensor, pressure sensor, fans, and thermistors.
- Other components like resistor, capacitor, transistor, voltage regulator, freewheeling diode, LED, connecting wire etc. also required for project which are provide by University. Other useful website to purchase component are eBay, microchip, maxim, RS.

Name of Components	Market Cost (£/unit)	Availability
Micro PIC	--	Provided by University
DS18B20	1.90	Provided by University
SHT11	19.17	Provided by University

MAX3232CPE	1.86	Provided by University
PWM FANS	36.57	Provided by University
MPX4115A	9.09	Provided by University
PCB board	3.00	Provided by University

References

[1] Giau Nguyen, "Sandstorm project monitoring the environment inside the chamber", 2nd year report, Northumbria University.

[2] A. K. Majumdar, J. C. Ricklin, "Free Space Laser Communications Principles and Advances", Springer ISBN 978-0-387-28652-5, 2008.

[3] H. Hemmati, "Near-Earth Laser Communications", California, Taylor & Francis Group, Book, LLC, 2008.

[4] H. Willebrand and B. S. Ghuman, "Free-Space Optics Enabling Optical Connectivity in Today's Networks", SAMS, 0-672-32248-x, 2002.

[5] B. Olivieret, et al., "Free-Space Optics, Propagation and Communication", Book, ISTE, 2006. 6] Roberto Ramirez-Iniguez, Sevia M. Idrus and Ziran Sun, "Optical Wireless Communications IR for Wireless Connectivity", Taylor & Francis Group, Book, CRC Press, 2007.

[7] N. Araki, H. Yashima, "A Channel Model of Optical Wireless Communications during Rainfall", IEEE, 0-7803-9206, 2005.

[8] Z. Ghassemlooy and W. O. Popoola , "Terrestrial Free Space Optical Communication" , Optical Communications Research Group, NCR Lab., Northumbia University, Newcastle upon Tyne, UK, 2010.

[9] Nadia B. M. Nawawi, "Wireless Local Area Network System Employing Free Space Optic Communication Link", A Bachelor Degree thesis, May 2009.

[10] Delower H. and Golam S. A., "Performance Evaluation of the Free Space Optical (FSO) Communication with the Effects of the atmospheric Turbulence", A Bachelor Degree thesis, January 2008.

11] M. Zaatari, "Wireless Optical Communications Systems in Enterprise Networks", the Telecommunications Review, 2003.

[12] I. I. Kim, B. McArthur and E. Korevaar, "Comparison of laser beam propagation at 785 nm and 1550 nm in fog and haze for optical wireless communications", Optical Wireless Communications III, SPIE, 4214, 2001.

[13] Jeganathan, Muthu and Pavellonov, "Multi-Gigabits per Second Optical Wireless Communications", 2000.

[14] Bloom S. E. Korevaar, J. Schuster, H. Willebrand, "Understanding the Performance of Free Space Optics", Journal of Optical Networking, 2003.

[15] Alexander S. B., "Optical Communication Receiver Design", (ISOE) SPIE, 1997.

[16] D. Romain, M. Larkin, G. Ghayel, B. Paulson and g. Nykolak , "Optical wireless propagation, theory vs. Experiment", Optical Wireless Communication III, Proc. SPIE, Vol.4214, 2001.

[17] W. E. K. Middleton, "Vision through the Atmosphere", University of Toronto Press, Toronto, 1963.

[18] I. I. Kim, B. McArthur, and E. Korevaar, "Comparison of laser beam propagation at 785 nm and 1550 nm in fog and haze for optical wireless communications", Proc. SPIE, 4214, pp. 26-37, 2000.

[19] S. G. Narasimhan and S. K. Nayar, "Vision and the Atmosphere", 2007.

[20] B. Naimullah, S. Hitam, N. Shah, M. Othman and S. Anas, "Analysis of the Effect of Haze on Free Space Optical Communication in the Malaysian Environment", IEEE, 2007.

[21] F. T. Arecchi, E. O. Schulz-Dubois, "Laser Handbook". North-Holland publishing Co; 3 Reprint edition (Dec 1972)

[22] Willebrand, Heinz A., Ghuman B. S. "Fiber Optic Without Fiber Light Pointe Communications", 2001.

[23] N. J Veck, "Atmospheric Transmission and Natural Illumination (visible to microwave

regions) ", GEC Journal of Research, 3(4), pp. 209 – 223, 1985.

[24] M. A. Bramson, "in Infrared Radiation", A handbook for Applications, Plenum Press, p. 602, 1969.

[25] Earl J. McCartney, "Optics of the Atmosphere: Scattering by Molecules and Particles", Wiley & Sons, New York, 1997.

[26] B. Bova, S. Rudnicki, "The Story of Light", Source book ISBN, 2001.

[27] P. P. Smyth et. al., "Optical Wireless Local Area Networks Enabling Technologies", BT Technology Journal, 11(2), pp. 56–64, 1993.

[28] M. S. Awan, L. C. Horwath, S. S. Muhammad, E. Leitgeb, F. Nadeem, M. S. Khan, "Characterization of Fog and Snow Attenuations for Free-Space Optical Propagation", Journal, Vol. 4, No. 8, 2009

[29] Achour M., "Simulating Atmospheric Free-Space Optical Propagation part I, Haze, Fog and Low Clouds, Rainfall Attenuation", Optical Wireless Communications, Proceedings of SPIE, 2002.

[30] I. Kim, R. et. al. , "Wireless Optical Transmission of Fast Ethernet, FDDI, ATM, and ESCON Protocol Data using the Terra Link Laser Communication System" , Opt. Eng. , 37 , pp. 3143-3155 , 1998.

[31] N Gondhalekar, " Project Planning Report", Nov 2012,Northumbria University

www.ingramcontent.com/pod-product-compliance
Lightning Source LLC
LaVergne TN
LVHW042257060326
832902LV00009B/1087